Collins
PICTURE ATLAS

ILLUSTRATED BY STEVE EVANS

PICTURE ATLAS

Published by Collins
An imprint of HarperCollins Publishers
Westerhill Road
Bishopbriggs
Glasgow G64 2QT
www.harpercollins.co.uk

First edition 2015

ISBN 978-0-00-811539-5

10 9 8 7 6 5 4 3 2 1

Printed and bound in Hong Kong

Collins Bartholomew, the UK's leading independent geographical
information supplier, can provide a digital, custom, and
premium mapping service to a variety of markets.
For further information:
Tel: +44 (0)208 307 4515
e-mail: collinsbartholomew@harpercollins.co.uk

Visit our websites at:
www.collins.co.uk or www.collinsbartholomew.com

If you would like to comment on any aspect of this book, please contact
us at the above address, online or email us at address below.

e-mail: collinsmaps@harpercollins.co.uk

CONTENTS

World

NORTH
AMERICA

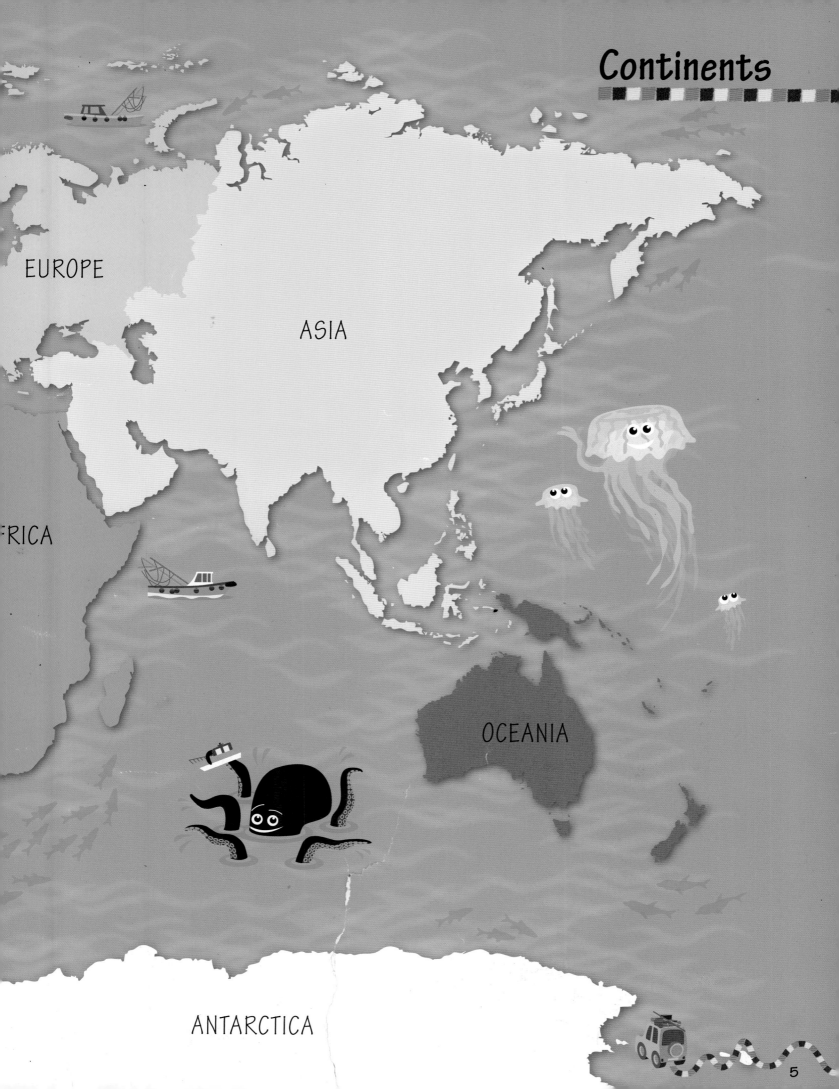

Continents

EUROPE

ASIA

FRICA

OCEANIA

ANTARCTICA

World

GREENLAND

ICELAND

N

CANADA

IRELAND

UNITED KINGDOM

FRANC

PORTUGAL   SPAIN

UNITED STATES
OF AMERICA

ATLANTIC OCEAN

MOROCCO

ALGERIA

MEXICO

CUBA

MAURITANIA   MALI

JAMAICA

SENEGAL

BURKINA
FASO

GUATEMALA

NICARAGUA

GUINEA

COSTA RICA

PACIFIC OCEAN

GHANA

CA

VENEZUELA

GUYANA
SURINAME

COLOMBIA

ECUADOR

PERU

BRAZIL

BOLIVIA

PARAGUAY

CHILE

URUGUAY

ARGENTINA

Countries

ARCTIC OCEAN

PEN

FINLAND

ESTONIA

LATVIA

ND

BELARUS

UKRAINE

ROMANIA

BULGARIA

GREECE

TURKEY

SYRIA

IRAQ

EGYPT

SAUDI ARABIA

OMAN

SUDAN

ERITREA

YEMEN

RAL CAN IC

SOUTH SUDAN

ETHIOPIA

OCRATIC PUBLIC HE CONGO

KENYA

SOMALIA

TANZANIA

ZAMBIA

MOZAMBIQUE

ZIMBABWE

TSWANA

MADAGASCAR

TH AFRICA

RUSSIA

KAZAKHSTAN

MONGOLIA

TURKMENISTAN

AFGHANISTAN

IRAN

PAKISTAN

NEPAL

INDIA

BANGLADESH

CHINA

MYANMAR (BURMA)

THAILAND

VIETNAM

SRI LANKA

MALAYSIA

NORTH KOREA

SOUTH KOREA

JAPAN

TAIWAN

PHILIPPINES

INDONESIA

PAPUA NEW GUINEA

SOLOMON ISLANDS

VANUATU

FIJI

NEW CALEDONIA

INDIAN OCEAN

PACIFIC OCEAN

AUSTRALIA

NEW ZEALAND

SOUTHERN OCEAN

ANTARCTICA

World

ARCTIC OCEAN

PACIFIC OCEAN

INDIAN OCEAN

SOUTHERN OCEAN

Europe

ICELAND

ATLANTIC OCEAN

NORWAY

DENMARK

UNITED KINGDOM

IRELAND

NETHERLANDS

BELGIUM

GERMANY

LUXEMBOURG

CZECH REPUBLIC

POLAND

AUSTRIA

SWITZERLAND

SLOVENIA

CROATIA

Europe is the world's second smallest continent. It is bordered by the Arctic Ocean to the north, the Atlantic Ocean to the west and the Mediterranean Sea to the south.

FRANCE

BOSNIA HERZEGO

ITALY

MONTENE

SPAIN

ANDORRA

PORTUGAL

MEDITERRAN

ARCTIC OCEAN

FINLAND

RUSSIA

ESTONIA

LATVIA

LITHUANIA

A

BELARUS

UKRAINE

MOLDOVA

ROMANIA

BULGARIA

DONIA

CE

11

Northern

An ocean current called the Gulf Stream brings mild, wet weather to parts of Northern Europe. Winters in the far north can be very cold, with temperatures as low as -50°C.

Iceland

Hammerfest

Scandinavia

Ben Nevis

Welcome to lavaland! **Iceland** has over 100 volcanoes and one third of all the lava flows on Earth.

Hammerfest is one of the most northerly towns in the world. Wild reindeer often wander along the streets.

Ben Nevis is the highest mountain in the United Kingdom. It is 1344 metres (4409 feet) high and you can see for miles from the top - if it isn't cloudy!

Lots of stories are told about trolls in **Scandinavia**. Trolls can be ugly, messy, nasty creatures that live in caves or forests. They turn to stone if sunlight hits them.

Southern

The Mediterranean Sea has been crossed by merchants and travellers for thousands of years. The ancient empires of Rome and Greece developed on its shores.

Mont Blanc is on the border between France and Italy. It is the highest peak in the Alps mountain range. There are lots of ski resorts nearby.

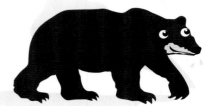

Ice cream, which is known in **Italy** as gelato, was invented in Naples. Italy is also the home of pizza!

The brown bear is the largest predator in Europe. Even though it is very big, it can run very fast. How fast do you think it could ski?

Mont Blanc

Spain

Italy

In **Spain** the tooth fairy gets her friend Ratoncito Pérez, the tooth mouse, to collect children's teeth.

TURKEY

CYPRUS
LEBANON
SYRIA
ISRAEL
JORDAN
IRAQ
KUWAIT

SAUDI
ARABIA
BAHRAIN
QATAR
UNITED ARAB
EMIRATES

YEMEN

OMAN

GEORGIA
ARMENIA   AZERBAIJAN

TURKMENISTAN

UZBEKISTAN

TAJIKISTAN

KYRGYZSTAN

KAZAKHSTAN

AFGHANISTAN

PAKISTAN

NEPAL   BHUTAN

BANGLADESH

INDIA

SRI LANKA

MON

CHINA

LAOS

THAILAN

CA

INDIAN OCEAN

Asia

PACIFIC OCEAN

RUSSIA

NORTH
KOREA

SOUTH
KOREA

JAPAN

Asia is the world's largest continent
and more people live here than in
any other continent. It covers about
one third of the land on Earth.

TAIWAN

CAMBODIA

VIETNAM

PHILIPPINES

MALAYSIA

BRUNEI

MALAYSIA

SINGAPORE

PHILIPPINES

INDONESIA

MALAYSIA

EAST TIMOR

17

Asia

Afghanistan

Saudi Arabia

Dubai

Saudi Arabia has one fifth of all the oil in the world. The oil lies deep underground and wells are drilled to pump it out.

Camel racing is one of the oldest sports in South West Asia. Camels can run nearly as fast as horses. At the Al Marmoum racetrack in **Dubai**, children used to be the jockeys but now they use robots instead!

South West and South Asia

The world's first civilizations formed in Western Asia. There are large areas of desert, but also vast expanses of forest and fertile valleys.

Snow leopards live in the cold north of **Afghanistan**. Their thick fur keeps them warm. Red giant flying squirrels live in the warmer south. They don't really fly but glide from tree to tree.

The horned viper snake has spiky scales on its snout that poke up like a horn. It has long fangs and a poisonous bite.

China and Japan

China is the third largest country in the world, after Russia and Canada. Japan is made up of nearly 7000 islands. It is one of the most densely populated countries in the world.

China

Japan

When it stands up, the Sarus crane is as tall as an adult. The red-crowned crane is the national bird of **China**.

The most popular sport in **Japan** is baseball.

Dragons are mythical creatures that appear in many different cultures. In **China**, the dragon is a symbol of wisdom, power and luck.

The Great Wall of China is the longest man-made structure in the world. It is an incredible 8850 kilometres (5500 miles) long. That's further than the distance between New York and Moscow!

Snow monkeys, also called Japanese macaques, often make snowballs for fun, just like us!

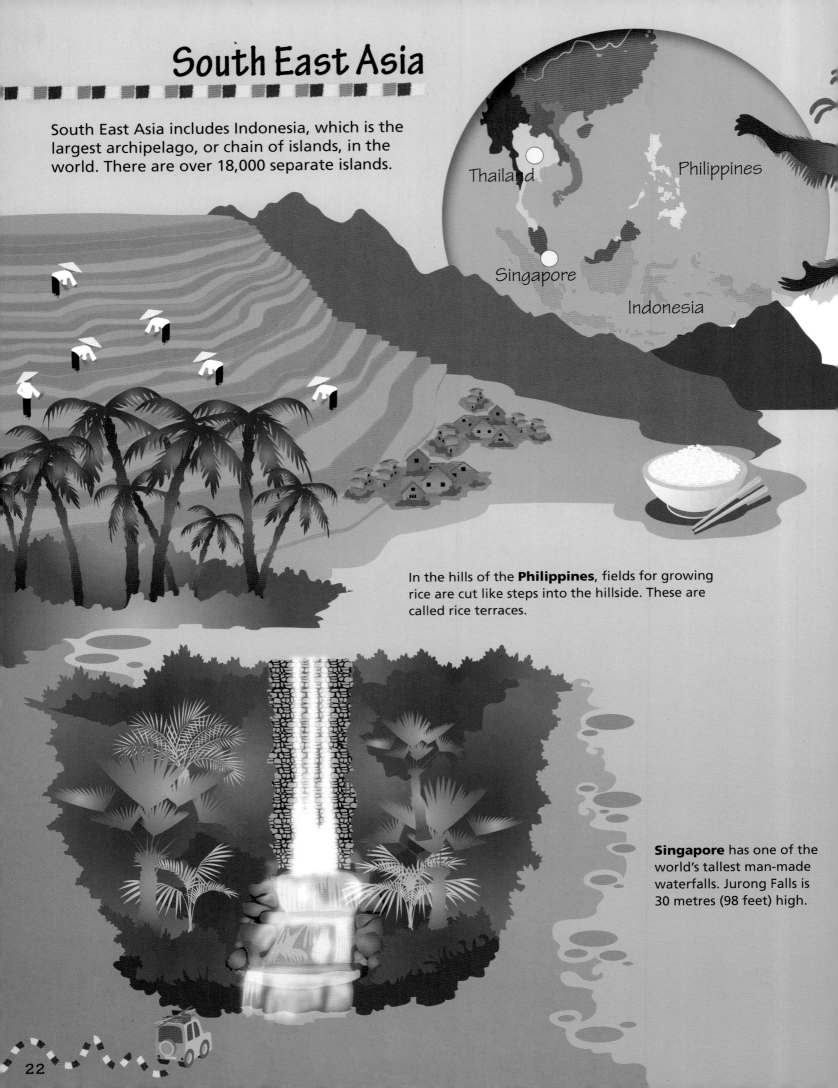

South East Asia

South East Asia includes Indonesia, which is the largest archipelago, or chain of islands, in the world. There are over 18,000 separate islands.

Thailand

Philippines

Singapore

Indonesia

In the hills of the **Philippines**, fields for growing rice are cut like steps into the hillside. These are called rice terraces.

Singapore has one of the world's tallest man-made waterfalls. Jurong Falls is 30 metres (98 feet) high.

Asia

Indonesia has 167 active volcanoes. There are also lots of earthquakes, and sometimes there are several tremors in one day.

Many houses in river valleys in **Thailand** are built on stilts. This stops them being flooded by the heavy monsoon rains.

Africa

ERITREA

DJIBOUTI

ETHIOPIA

SOMALIA

SOUTH SUDAN

UGANDA

SUDAN

EGYPT

CHAD

CENTRAL AFRICAN REPUBLIC

CAMEROON

OS

EQUATORIAL GUINEA

NIGER

NIGERIA

LIBYA

TUNISIA

BENIN

TOGO

GHANA

BURKINA FASO

CÔTE D'IVOIRE

ALGERIA

MALI

LIBERIA

SIERRA LEONE

GUINEA

GUINEA-BISSAU

THE GAMBIA

SENEGAL

MAURITANIA

WESTERN SAHARA

MOROCCO

INDIAN OCEAN

MADAGASCAR

BURUNDI

TANZANIA

MALAWI

MOZAMBIQUE

OF THE CONGO

ZAMBIA

ZIMBABWE

ANGOLA

SWAZILAND

SOUTH AFRICA

LESOTHO

BOTSWANA

NAMIBIA

ANGOLA

ATLANTIC OCEAN

Africa is the second largest continent on Earth. Europe could fit into Africa nearly three times!

Northern Africa

Northern Africa is dominated by the Sahara Desert. The snow-capped Atlas mountains are near the coast and separate the Sahara and the Mediterranean Sea.

The **Sahara Desert** is the world's largest sandy desert. It covers an area larger than Brazil. Some of its sand dunes are as tall as buildings.

Africa

Sahara
Desert

Egypt

Sudan

Nile

Egypt is famous for its pyramids, but there are actually many more of them in **Sudan**.

The **Nile** is the longest river in the world. It is 6695 kilometres (4160 miles) long. Eleven countries get water from it and its tributaries.

Four of the five fastest land animals live in Africa: the cheetah, the wildebeest, the lion and the Thomson's gazelle. The cheetah is the fastest, with a top speed of 120 kilometres per hour (75 miles per hour).

Central and Southern Africa

The landscapes of central and southern Africa are very varied. They range from thick jungle to forest, grasslands and desert. There are high mountains, fertile valleys and low-lying coastal areas.

Lake Victoria

South Africa

The African elephant is the world's largest living land animal. It can weigh up to 7 tonnes - that's as heavy as five family cars! Flapping their big ears keeps them cool.

Africa

The Baobab tree is a familiar sight on the African grasslands. It grows in 32 countries across the continent and can live for 5000 years. Africans call the Baobab the 'tree of life' and use it in many traditional remedies.

The Nile River flows from **Lake Victoria**, which is the biggest lake in Africa and the second largest freshwater lake in the world.

Some of the most amazing large animals on Earth live in **South Africa**, including the giraffe, hippopotamus, leopard and lion.

North America

CANADA

PACIFIC OCEAN

HOLLYWOOD

UNITED STATES OF AMERICA

LAS VEGAS

MEXICO

HAWAII

GUATEMALA
EL SAL

30

GREENLAND

ATLANTIC OCEAN

North America consists of over twenty countries, the largest being Canada. North America is home to over 500 million people. The most populated city is Mexico City. Almost 9 million people live there.

THE BAHAMAS

CUBA

DOMINICAN REPUBLIC

HAITI

PUERTO RICO

JAMAICA

NICARAGUA

PANAMA

Diner

Canada and USA

Canada is the world's second largest country and has the longest coastline at 202,080 kilometres (125,570 miles). The USA is the world's fourth largest country. The tallest mountain in North America is in the state of Alaska in the USA. It is called Mount McKinley and it is 6168 metres (20,237 feet) high.

The **Statue of Liberty** was designed by a French sculptor and built in France. The statue was shipped across the Atlantic Ocean in 350 pieces packed in crates. It was then assembled like a giant 3-D jigsaw puzzle and declared open in 1886.

Some bristlecone pine trees are more than 5000 years old. This makes them some of the world's oldest living things. These trees grow in high, dry places in the western USA.

North America

Humans first walked on the moon in 1969. The first person to step onto the lunar surface was an American called Neil Armstrong. Another astronaut played golf on the moon!

A mysterious creature called Ogopogo is said to live in **Lake Okanagan** in Canada. Those who have seen it say it is 15 metres (50 feet) long and has many humps - a bit like the Loch Ness Monster.

Canada

Lake Okanagan

USA

Statue of Liberty

Mexico and the Caribbean

The Caribbean is made up of thousands of tropical islands which are often hit by hurricanes. In Southern Mexico, near the Caribbean Sea, it is hot and humid, but northern Mexico is cooler, and dry and rocky.

The volcano rabbit lives in **Mexico**. These brave bunnies are very rare and can be spotted on only four volcanoes.

occy
Milk Chocolate
and smooth cacao

If you like chocolate, you have **Mexico** to thank. Chocolate is made from the seeds of the cacao tree, and was first enjoyed here 3000 years ago. Corn and chillies are also from Mexico.

North America

Mexico

Caribbean

Dominica

There are thousands of islands in the **Caribbean**, but very few have people living on them.

Trafalgar Falls in **Dominica** are unique twin waterfalls - one is hot and one is cold. Like giant taps! There are natural hot springs at the bottom where you can swim.

Hot

Cold

South America

South America is home to almost 400 million people. It is made up of 12 countries.

TRINIDAD & TOBAGO

GUYANA

SURINAME

FRENCH GUIANA

VENEZUELA

COLOMBIA

BRAZIL

ECUADOR

PERU

BOLIVIA

GALAPAGOS ISLANDS (ECUADOR)

ATLANTIC OCEAN

SOUTH GEORGIA (UK)

URUGUAY

ARGENTINA

FALKLAND ISLANDS (UK)

CHILE

PACIFIC OCEAN

Easter Island

South America

Anacondas are some of the largest and heaviest snakes in the world. They live in the **Amazon Basin**, and sneak up on prey as large as goats, which they swallow whole.

Machu Picchu is a mountain-top city built 500 years ago by the native Incas. Nobody knows for sure why they abandoned it 100 years later.

Angel Falls

Amazon Basin

Manaus-Iranduba Bridge

Machu Picchu

North

Most people in this area live on the low-lying land near the coast. Potatoes, peppers and beans have been grown here for thousands of years.

More water flows in the Amazon than in any other river on Earth. It contains more water than the seven next largest rivers combined. The Amazon mostly flows through dense, remote jungle and there is only one bridge crossing it, the **Manaus-Iranduba Bridge** in Brazil.

Angel Falls in Venezuela is the world's highest waterfall. It is 979 metres (3212 feet) high. Water from the top takes 15 seconds to reach the ground. The waterfall lies deep in the jungle and was only discovered in 1933.

South America

Llamas are very useful to people in the **Andes** mountains. They carry baggage, provide meat and their soft wool makes warm clothes. Just don't annoy them - they'll spit at you!

Easter Island

Chile

Andes

Patagonia

Uruguay

Buenos Aires

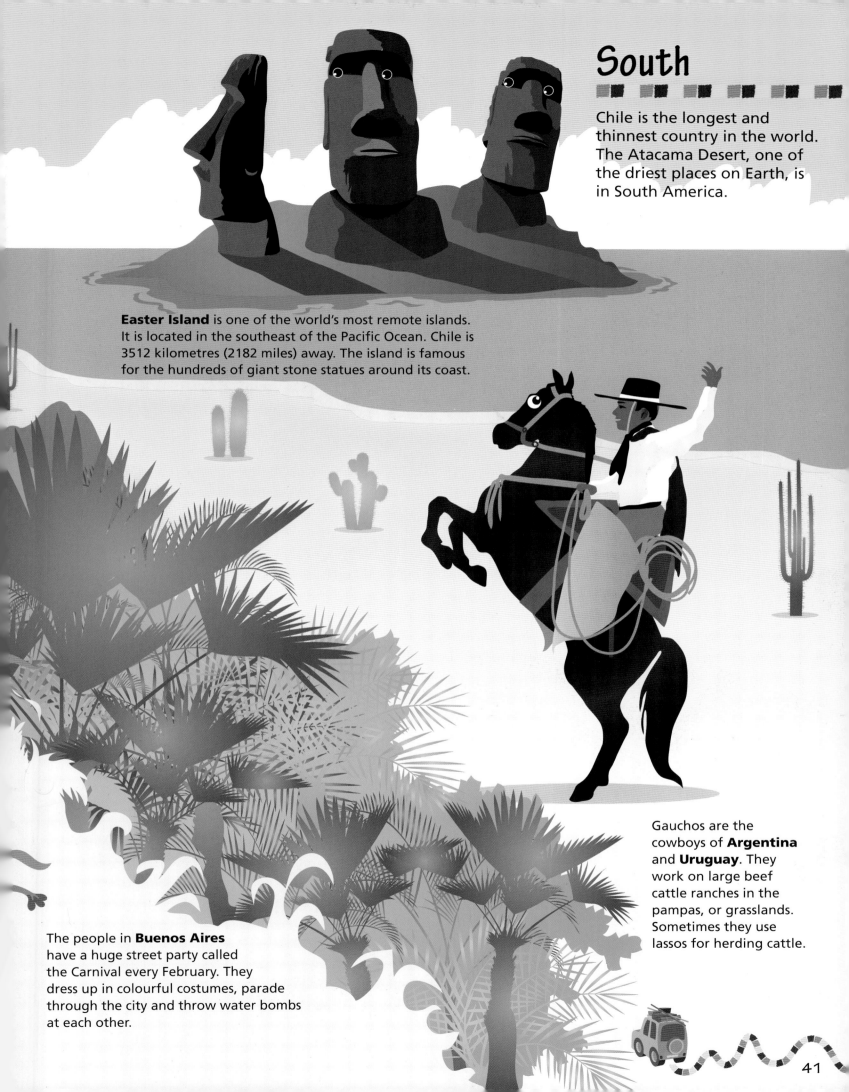

South

Chile is the longest and thinnest country in the world. The Atacama Desert, one of the driest places on Earth, is in South America.

Easter Island is one of the world's most remote islands. It is located in the southeast of the Pacific Ocean. Chile is 3512 kilometres (2182 miles) away. The island is famous for the hundreds of giant stone statues around its coast.

Gauchos are the cowboys of **Argentina** and **Uruguay**. They work on large beef cattle ranches in the pampas, or grasslands. Sometimes they use lassos for herding cattle.

The people in **Buenos Aires** have a huge street party called the Carnival every February. They dress up in colourful costumes, parade through the city and throw water bombs at each other.

41

INDIAN OCEAN

AUSTRALIA

INDIAN PACIFIC

Oceania

Oceania is the world's smallest and flattest continent. It has the world's largest coral reef called the Great Barrier Reef. New Zealand has two main islands - North Island and South Island.

PAPUA NEW GUINEA

SOLOMON ISLANDS

VANUATU

FIJI

NEW CALEDONIA (France)

PACIFIC OCEAN

NEW ZEALAND

Oceania

The remote **Kimberley region** of Western Australia has one of the world's largest diamond mines. It is famous for its pink diamonds.

The Tasmanian Devil's powerful neck muscles give it one of the strongest bites of any living mammal. It also has a deafening screech.

The **Great Barrier Reef** is the world's largest living structure. It is over 2300 kilometres (1499 miles) long and can be seen from space. The reef is made of billions of tiny creatures called coral polyps.

Kimberley region

Great Barrier Reef

New Zealand

Tasmania

New Zealand has 4 million people and 30 million sheep. That means that for every person there are over 7 sheep.

Australia and New Zealand

45

Antarctica

Antarctica is the coldest, driest and windiest continent. It is nearly twice the size of Australia and is almost completely covered in ice.

Penguins only live in the Southern Hemisphere. King Penguins are one of the largest penguin species, reaching 100 centimetres tall. They have four layers of feathers to stay warm on the cold islands near Antarctica where they live.

The Antarctic ice cap is bigger than the USA! It contains nearly all of the ice found on Earth, and is nearly 5 kilometres (3 miles) thick. If the Antarctic ice sheet melted, sea levels would rise by 60 metres (200 feet).

It is too cold for people to live comfortably in Antarctica. Only scientists working in special research stations stay there.

Although it's icy, Antarctica is the world's largest desert because it doesn't rain or snow very often. In the Dry Valleys region it hasn't rained for 2 million years.

SOUTHERN OCEAN

SOUTH AMERICA

ANTARCTICA

ANTARCTIC PENINSULA

RONNE ICE SHELF

FILCHNER ICE SHELF

ROSS ICE SHELF

SOUTH POLE

DRY VALLEYS

SOUTHERN OCEAN

The Arctic Ocean

The Arctic Ocean is mostly covered by sea ice in winter. Some of this melts in summer. There is no land at the North Pole, only ice.

Icebreakers don't plough through pack ice - they use their power and sloping bow to ride up onto it. Gravity then does the hard work, pulling the heavy ship down and breaking the ice.

Polar bears are only found in the Arctic and are the largest land predators in the world. They have black skin and although their fur appears white, the hairs are actually see-through.

CANADA

RUSSIA

ARCTIC OCEAN

NORTH POLE

GREENLAND

SCANDINAVIA

Grey whales migrate further than any other mammal. They swim from their Arctic feeding grounds to the warm waters of the Gulf of Mexico to mate and give birth. That's a 20,000 kilometre (12,500 mile) round trip every year.

Walruses can stay underwater for up to 30 minutes. They have whiskers and long tusks, which can reach 1 m (3 ft 3 in). Walruses use them for making holes in ice, climbing out of the water and for fighting.

INDEX